1986

DAILY HOROSCOPE

DAILY HOROSCOPE

POEMS BY

DANA GIOIA

• • •

GRAYWOLF PRESS : SAINT PAUL

2 4 6 8 9 7 5 3
First printing 1986

Published by GRAYWOLF PRESS
Post Office Box 75006
Saint Paul, Minnesota 55175

· ACKNOWLEDGMENTS ·

These poems, sometimes in earlier versions, appeared in the following publications: *Boulevard*: "An Emigré in Autumn"; *Cumberland Poetry Review*: "The Burning Ladder"; *The Hudson Review*: "An Elegy for Vladimir de Pachmann," "Lives of the Great Composers," "God Only Knows," "Daily Horoscope," "His Three Women," "Parts of Summer Weather," "View from the Second Story," "Photograph of My Mother as a Young Girl," "Eastern Standard Time," "A Short History of Tobacco," "The End of a Season," "In Cheever Country"; *New England Review*: "Song from a Courtyard Window"; *The New Yorker*: "Garden on the Campagna," "California Hills in August," "Speech from a Novella," "In Chandler Country"; *The Ontario Review*: "Bix Beiderbecke," "Insomnia"; *Paris Review*: "Flying over Clouds"; *Pequod*: "Waiting in the Airport," "Instructions for the Afternoon"; *Poetry*: "My Secret Life," "The Journey, the Arrival and the Dream," "Cuckoos," "Thanks for Remembering Us," "The Sunday News," "The Country Wife," "Cruising with the Beachboys," "The End"; *The Poetry Review*: "The Room Upstairs"; *Sequoia*: "The Mad Nun," "The Letter"; *Southwest Review*: "Pornotopia," "Four Speeches for Pygmalion"; *The Threepenny Review*: "The Man in the Open Doorway"; *Vanderbilt Poetry Review*: "A Curse on Geographers."

Some poems were also reprinted in limited-edition chapbooks or broadsides by the following presses: *Aralia Press*: "View from the Second Story," "Insomnia"; *Bowery Press* (New York Center for Book Arts): TWO POEMS; *Ex Ophidia*: JOURNEYS IN SUNLIGHT; *The Press at Colorado College*: "Sunday Night in Santa Rosa"; *The Windhover Press*: DAILY HOROSCOPE.

"Sunday Night in Santa Rosa" first appeared in the anthology, *A Green Place*, edited by William Jay Smith.

"The Sunday News," "Bix Beiderbecke" and "Photograph of My Mother as a Young Girl" also appeared in the 1984 edition of *Anthology of Magazine Verse & Yearbook of American Poetry*. "Parts of Summer Weather" and "Speech from a Novella" appeared in the 1985 edition.

The author thanks these editors and printers for their generous support.

FOR MY PARENTS

Michael Gioia & Dorothy Ortez Gioia

Al cor gentil ripara sempre Amore

· CONTENTS ·

I.

II. Daily Horoscope

III.

IV. Journeys in Sunlight

V.

· I ·

THE BURNING LADDER

Jacob
never climbed the ladder
burning in his dream. Sleep
pressed him like a stone
in the dust,
and when
he should have risen
like a flame to join
that choir, he was sick
of travelling,
and closed
his eyes to the Seraphim
ascending, unconscious
of the impossible distances
between their steps,
missed
them mount the brilliant
ladder, slowly disappearing
into the scattered light
between the stars,
slept
through it all, a stone
upon a stone pillow,
shivering. Gravity
always greater than desire.

CALIFORNIA HILLS IN AUGUST

I can imagine someone who found
these fields unbearable, who climbed
the hillside in the heat, cursing the dust,
cracking the brittle weeds underfoot,
wishing a few more trees for shade.

An Easterner especially, who would scorn
the meagerness of summer, the dry
twisted shapes of black elm,
scrub oak, and chaparral, a landscape
August has already drained of green.

One who would hurry over the clinging
thistle, foxtail, golden poppy,
knowing everything was just a weed,
unable to conceive that these trees
and sparse brown bushes were alive.

And hate the bright stillness of the noon
without wind, without motion,
the only other living thing
a hawk, hungry for prey, suspended
in the blinding, sunlit blue.

And yet how gentle it seems to someone
raised in a landscape short of rain –
the skyline of a hill broken by no more
trees than one can count, the grass,
the empty sky, the wish for water.

So strange to hear that song again tonight
Travelling on business in a rented car
Miles from anywhere I've been before.
And now a tune I haven't heard for years
Probably not since it last left the charts
Back in L.A. in 1969.
I can't believe I know the words by heart
And can't think of a girl to blame them on.

Every lovesick summer has its song,
And this one I pretended to despise,
But if I was alone when it came on,
I turned it up full-blast to sing along –
A primal scream in croaky baritone,
The notes all flat, the lyrics mostly slurred.
No wonder I spent so much time alone
Making the rounds in Dad's old Thunderbird.

Some nights I drove down to the beach to park
And walk along the railings of the pier.
The water down below was cold and dark,
The waves monotonous against the shore.
The darkness and the mist, the midnight sea,
The flickering lights reflected from the city –
A perfect setting for a boy like me,
The Cecil B. DeMille of my self-pity.

I thought by now I'd left those nights behind,
Lost like the girls that I could never get,

Gone with the years, junked with the old T-Bird.
But one old song, a stretch of empty road,
Can open up a door and let them fall
Tumbling like boxes from a dusty shelf,
Tightening my throat for no reason at all
Bringing on tears shed only for myself.

IN CHANDLER COUNTRY

California night. The Devil's wind,
the Santa Ana, blows in from the east,
raging through the canyon like a drunk
screaming in a bar.
                        The air tastes like
a stubbed-out cigarette. But why complain?
The weather's fine as long as you don't breathe.
Just lean back on the sweat-stained furniture,
lights turned out, windows shut against the storm,
and count your blessings.
                        Another sleepless night,
when every wrinkle in the bedsheet scratches
like a dry razor on a sunburned cheek,
when even ten-year whiskey tastes like sand,
and quiet women in the kitchen run
their fingers on the edges of a knife
and eye their husbands' necks. I wish them luck.

Tonight it seems that if I took the coins
out of my pocket and tossed them in the air
they'd stay a moment glistening like a net
slowly falling through dark water.
                        I remember
the headlights of the cars parked on the beach,
the narrow beams dissolving on the dark
surface of the lake, voices arguing
about the forms, the crackling radio,
the sheeted body lying on the sand,
the trawling net still damp beside it. No,

she wasn't beautiful – but at that age
when youth itself becomes a kind of beauty –
"Taking good care of your clients, Marlowe?"

Relentlessly the wind blows on. Next door
catching a scent, the dogs begin to howl.
Lean, furious, raw-eyed from the storm,
packs of coyotes come down from the hills
where there is nothing left to hunt.

EASTERN STANDARD TIME

Yesterday the clocks went back an hour,
and now, leaving work a little late,

I walk across the parking lot
where it's already dark and empty,

empty on a scale only the suburbs
could afford – thirty acres of smooth,

black asphalt, lined symmetrically by rows
of identical, bare-branched trees – tonight

more of an idea than a landscape,
a vast blueprint vandalized by autumn.

Shades of Callimachus, Coan ghosts of Philetas,
It is in your grove I would walk!

Instead I cross this familiar, stone-paved lot
feeling out of place, a Californian,

a stranger to the darker seasons,
walking through the end of an Eastern fall.

I have learned to tell
the changes that prefigure storms:

the heavy air, the circling wind
and graduate darkness, but still

each time the air goes through even these
accustomed changes, I grow uneasy.

Sudden storms, shifts in temperature, even snow
in midwinter still surprise me,

unable to feel at home in a landscape
so suddenly transformed.

Anxiety in Autumn! O Suburbs of Despair
where nothing but the weather ever changes!

Sometimes the saddest places in the world
are just the ordinary ones seen after hours.

Picture a department store at night
with the doors locked and lights turned off

or a beachhouse in the winter
dark and shuttered by the sea.

Walk through a stadium after the game
or even a parking lot everyone has left.

It's cold. The wind is blowing.
As far as I can see, there are leaves –

dry, brown, curling on themselves,
ankle-deep in places, and everywhere

sweeping across the numbered rows,
arranging and rearranging themselves,

some only to swirl up and fly away,
others to scratch along the asphalt.

They are alive! Swarming in movements
only they can understand.

And suddenly I realize the obvious:
that even this parking lot

was once a field. A field
sloping to the valley where now

the Interstate is running.
How much older they are, the leaves

just fallen
tracing out these shapes from memory.

MEN AFTER WORK

Done with work, they are sitting by themselves
in coffeeshops or diners, taking up the booths,
filling every other seat along the counter,
waiting for the menu, for the water,
for the girl to come and take their order,
always on the edge of words, almost without appetite,
knowing there is nothing on the menu that they want,
waiting patiently to ask for one
more refill of their coffee, surprised
that even its bitterness will not wake them up.
Still they savour it, holding each sip
lukewarm in their mouths, this last taste of evening.

WAITING IN THE AIRPORT

On the same journey each of them
Is going somewhere else. A goose-necked
Woman in a flowered dress
Stares gravely at two businessmen.
They turn away but carry on
Their argument on real estate.

Lost in a mist of aftershave,
A salesman in a brown toupée
Is scribbling on his *Racing Form*
While a fat man stares down at his hands
As if there should be something there.

The soldiers stand in line for sex –
With wives or girlfriends, whoever
They hope is waiting for them at
The other end. The wrapped perfume,
The bright, stuffed animals they clutch
Tremble under so much heat.

Lives have been pulled cross-continent.
So much will soon be going on
But somewhere else – divorces, birthdays,
Deaths and million-dollar deals.

But nothing ever happens here,
This terminal that narrows to
A single unattended gate,
One entrance to so many worlds.

No earthly image – only clouds,
affluent clouds, seen from high above,
still bright at the approach of evening.

Soft valleys hidden in a snowdrift,
waterfalls of ice and air,
not whiteness but a dream of whiteness,
an innocence one may have felt
on earth – but only for a moment,

waking unexpectedly at dawn
one winter morning after a storm
to find the shabby blacktopped streets
immaculate in sunlight, glossed
by deep smooth banks of snow, before
the earliest car or footfall.

              So strange,
this world the ancients never saw,
and yet their words now come to mind,
nimbus, cirrus, cumuli,
magic names to summon all
the scattered elements of air.

O paradise beyond the glass,
beyond our touch, cast and recast,
shifting in wind. Delicate world
of air too thin to breathe, of cold
beyond endurance.

                    And nothingness
that mirrors our desire – not of death
but of your fluent oblivion,
of insubstantial dusk and dawn,
your whiteness burning in the sun.

The plane flies westward gaining time.
The dark recedes – and up ahead
the sky is cloudless, clear, and bright.

THE MAN IN THE OPEN DOORWAY

This is the world in which he lives:
Four walls, a desk, a swivel chair,
A doorway with no door to close,
Vents to bring in air.

There are two well-marked calendars,
Some pencils, and a telephone
The women at the front desk answer
Leaving him alone.

There is a clock he hardly sees
Beside the window on the wall.
It moves in only one direction,
Never stops at all.

Outside the February wind
Scrapes up against the windowpane,
And a blue-green land is fading,
Scarred by streaks of rain.

The phones go off. The files are locked.
But the doorway still is lit at night
Like the tall window of a church
Bleached in winter light.

Sometimes the shadow of his hand
Falls from his desk onto the wall
And is the only thing that moves
Anywhere at all.

Or else he will drive back at night
To walk along the corridor
And, thinking of the day's success,
Trace his steps once more,

Then pause in a darkened stairway
Until the sounds of his steps have ceased
And stroke the wall as if it were
Some attendant beast.

INSOMNIA

Now you hear what the house has to say.
Pipes clanking, water running in the dark,
the mortgaged walls shifting in discomfort,
and voices mounting in an endless drone
of small complaints like the sounds of a family
that year by year you've learned how to ignore.

But now you must listen to the things you own,
all that you've worked for these past years,
the murmur of property, of things in disrepair,
the moving parts about to come undone,
and twisting in the sheets remember all
the faces you could not bring yourself to love.

How many voices have escaped you until now,
the venting furnace, the floorboards underfoot,
the steady accusations of the clock
numbering the minutes no one will mark.
The terrible clarity this moment brings,
the useless insight, the unbroken dark.

IN CHEEVER COUNTRY

Half an hour north of Grand Central
the country opens up. Through the rattling
grime-streaked windows of the coach, streams appear,
pine trees gather into woods, and the leaf-swept yards
grow large enough to seem picturesque.

Farther off smooth parkways curve along the rivers,
trimmed by well-kept trees, and the County Airport
now boasts seven lines, but to know this country
see it from a train — even this crowded local
jogging home half an hour before dark

smelling of smoke and rain-damp shoes
on an afternoon of dodging sun and showers.
One trip without a book or paper
will show enough to understand
this landscape no one takes too seriously.

The architecture of each station still preserves
its fantasy beside the sordid tracks —
defiant pergolas, a shuttered summer lodge,
a shadowy pavilion framed by high-arched windows
in this land of northern sun and lingering winter.

The town names stenciled on the platform signs —
Clear Haven, Bullet Park, and Shady Hill —
show that developers at least believe in poetry
if only as a talisman against the commonplace.
There always seems so much to guard against.

The sunset broadens for a moment, and the passengers
standing on the platform turn strangely luminous
in the light streaming from the palisades across the river.
Some board the train. Others greet their arrivals
shaking hands and embracing in the dusk.

If there is an afterlife, let it be a small town
gentle as this spot at just this instant.
But the car doors close, and the bright crowd,
unaware of its election, disperses to the small
pleasures of the evening. The platform falls behind.

The train gathers speed. Stations are farther apart.
Marble staircases climb the hills where derelict estates
glimmer in the river-brightened dusk.
Some are convents now, some orphanages,
these palaces the Robber Barons gave to God.

And some are merely left to rot where now
broken stone lions guard a roofless colonnade,
a half-collapsed gazebo bursts with tires,
and each detail warns it is not so difficult
to make a fortune as to pass it on.

But splendor in ruins is splendor still,
even glimpsed from a passing train,
and it is wonderful to imagine standing
in the balustraded gardens above the river
where barges still ply their distant commerce.

Somewhere upstate huge factories melt ore,
mills weave fabric on enormous looms,
and sweeping combines glean the cash-green fields.
Fortunes are made. Careers advance like armies.
But here so little happens that is obvious.

Here in the odd light of a rainy afternoon
a ledger is balanced and put away,
a houseguest knots his tie beside a bed,
and a hermit thrush sings in the unsold lot
next to the tracks the train comes hurtling down.

Finally it's dark outside. Through the freight houses
and oil tanks the train begins to slow
approaching the station where rows of travel posters
and empty benches wait along the platform.
Outside a few cars idle in the sudden shower.

And this at last is home, this ordinary town
where the lights on the hill gleaming in the rain
are the lights that children bathe by, and it is time
to go home now – to drinks, to love, to supper,
to the modest places which contain our lives.

· II ·

DAILY
HOROSCOPE

in memory of Robert Fitzgerald

"Tu se' lo mio maestro, e il mio autore;
tu se' solo colui, da cui io tolsi
lo bello stile, che m'ha fatto onore."

INFERNO I, 85-87

Today will be like any other day.
You will wake to the familiar sounds
of the same hour in the same room,
sounds which no alarm is needed to announce.
And lying in the warm half-darkness, wish
for any of the dreams you left, convinced
that any change would be an argosy –
an hour's sleep, an unexpected visit.

But they are lost to you – the dreams, the sleep,
the faceless lovers you desire. Lost
as if your eyes were shut against the light,
and only these dull colors have remained,
the vision never coming into focus,
blurred or obscured this morning and forever.

Beyond your window, something like a wind
is filling in the emptiness of air.
Vast, hungry, and invisible, it sweeps
the morning clean of memories, then disappears.
The weather changes randomly. Rain
is falling from another planet
but cannot wash the daylight off
into familiar shapes. These walls, these streets,
this day can never be your home, and yet
there is no other world where you could live,
and so you will accept it.
                                        Just as others,
waking to sunlight and the sound of leaves,
accept the morning as their own, and walk
without surprise, through orchards crossed by streams,
where swift, cold water is running over stone.

Nothing is lost. Nothing is so small
that it does not return.
                              Imagine
that as a child on a day like this
you held a newly minted coin and had
the choice of spending it in any way
you wished.
                    Today the coin comes back to you,
the date rubbed out, the ancient mottoes vague,
the portrait covered with the dull shellac
of anything used up, passed on, disposed of
with something else in view, and always worth
a little less each time.
                              Now it returns,
and you will think it unimportant, lose
it in your pocket change as one more thing
that's not worth counting, not worth singling out.
That is the mistake you must avoid today.
You sent it on the journey to yourself.
Now hold it in your hand. Accept it as
the little you have earned today.
                              And realize
that you must choose again but over less.

Do not expect that if your book falls open
to a certain page, that any phrase
you read will make a difference today,
or that the voices you might overhear
when the wind moves through the yellow-green
and golden tent of autumn, speak to you.

Things ripen or go dry. Light plays on the
dark surface of the lake. Each afternoon
your shadow walks beside you on the wall,
and the days stay long and heavy underneath
the distant rumor of the harvest. One
more summer gone,
and one way or another you survive,
dull or regretful, never learning that
nothing is hidden in the obvious
changes of the world, that even the dim
reflection of the sun on tall, dry grass
is more than you will ever understand.

And only briefly then
you touch, you see, you press against
the surface of impenetrable things.

Beware of things in duplicate:
a set of knives, the cufflinks in a drawer,
the dice, the pair of Queens, the eyes
of someone sitting next to you.
Attend that empty minute in the evening
when looking at the clock, you see
its hands are fixed on the same hour
you noticed at your morning coffee.
These are the moments to beware
when there is nothing so familiar
or so close that it cannot betray you:
a twin, an extra key, an echo,
your own reflection in the glass.

The stars now rearrange themselves above you
but to no effect. Tonight,
only for tonight, their powers lapse,
and you must look toward earth. There will be
no comets now, no pointing star
to lead where you know you must go.

Look for smaller signs instead, the fine
disturbances of ordered things when suddenly
the rhythms of your expectation break
and in a moment's pause another world
reveals itself behind the ordinary.

And one small detail out of place will be
enough to let you know: a missing ring,
a breath, a footfall or a sudden breeze,
a crack of light beneath a darkened door.

News will arrive from far away: the phone
rings unexpectedly at night,
and a voice you almost recognize
will speak. Soft and familiar,
it mentions names you haven't heard for years,
names of another place, another time,
that street by street restore
the lost geography of childhood.
Half asleep you listen in the dark
gradually remembering where you are.
You start to speak. Then silence.
A dial tone. An intervening voice.
Or nothing. The call is finished.
Not even time to turn the lights on.
Now just the ticking of the clock,
the cold disorder of the bed.

• III •

PORNOTOPIA

Everyone has an entrance of his own.
While some prefer to step inside discreetly
From the French doors which look into the garden
Where as boys they watched their sisters bathe
In the sunlight, half hidden in the grass,
Others demand a formal introduction
And are driven to the door in limousines
Where valets take their cards, and as they enter,
Announce them to the crowd in thrilling tones.
Such differences are minor.
For whether they've imagined it to be
An isolated country house in England,
A columned, white colonial estate
Lined by palms against a tropic sky,
Or simply a well-furnished suite of rooms
In one of the city's better neighborhoods,
Once they have passed through the large, outer rooms,
The interiors are always the same.

AN ELEGY FOR VLADIMIR DE PACHMANN

(Odessa, 1848 – Rome, 1933)

"How absurd," cried the pianist de Pachmann
    to reporters from the *Minneapolis Dispatch*,
"that my talents or the talents of a Liszt
    were confined to so small a planet
as the earth. How much more could we have done
    given the dimensions of a fixed star?"
He began a prelude quietly, then stopped.
    "Once Chopin could play this well. Now only me."

When he brought his socks into the concert hall
    and dedicated that night's music to them,
or relearned his repertoire at sixty-nine
    using only the fourth and fifth fingers
of one hand, the critics thought his madness
    was theatrical, but the less learned
members of his audience, to whom he talked
    while playing, knew the truth.

Porters and impresarios told of coming on him,
    alone in a hotel suite, his back
curved like a monkey's, dancing and screeching
    in front of a dressing mirror,
or giving concerts for the velvet furniture
    in his room, knocking it together afterwards
for applause. "Dear friends," he whispered to it,
    "such love deserves an encore."

Now relegated to three short paragraphs
    in *Grove's Dictionary of Music*
and one out-of-stock recording of Chopin,
    he reappears only by schedule
in a few selections broadcast on his birthday,
    music produced by rolls on a mechanical piano
where no fingers touch the keys as each piece
    goes to its predictable finale.

Herr Bruckner often wandered into church
to join the mourners at a funeral.
The relatives of Berlioz were horrified.
"Such harmony," quoth Shakespeare, "is in
immortal souls....We cannot hear it." But
the radio is playing, and outside
rain splashes to the pavement. Now and then
the broadcast fails. On nights like these Schumann
would watch the lightning streak his windowpanes.

Outside the rain is falling on the pavement.
A scrap of paper tumbles down the street.
On rainy evenings Schumann jotted down
his melodies on windowpanes. "Such harmony!
We cannot hear it." The radio goes off and on.
At the rehearsal Gustav Holst exclaimed,
"I'm sick of music, especially my own!"
The relatives of Berlioz were horrified.
Haydn's wife used music to line pastry pans.

On rainy nights the ghost of Mendelssohn
brought melodies for Schumann to compose.
"Such harmony is in immortal souls....
We cannot hear it." One could suppose
Herr Bruckner would have smiled. At Tergensee
the peasants stood to hear young Paganini play,
but here there's lightning, and the thunder rolls.
The radio goes off and on. The rain
falls to the pavement like applause.

A scrap of paper tumbles down the street.
On rainy evenings Schumann would look out
and scribble on the windows of his cell.
"Such harmony." Cars splash out in the rain.
The relatives of Berlioz were horrified
to see the horses break from the cortege
and gallop with his casket to the grave.
Liszt wept to hear young Paganini play.
Haydn's wife used music to line pastry pans.

Here is the church,
Here is the steeple,
Open it up,
And see all the people.

God only knows

if Bach's greatest work
was just an improvised
accompaniment
between two verses of a hymn,
one that stopped the burghers
squirming in their pews
and made them not only
listen to the organ in the loft
but actually hear the roof
unbend itself
and leave the church wide
open to a terrifying sky
which he had filled with angels
holding ledgers
for a roll call of the damned,
whom they would have named,
had not the congregation
started up the final chorus
and sung

to save their souls.

A CURSE ON GEOGRAPHERS

We want an earth to walk upon,
Not reasons to remain at home.
Shall we make journeys only to see
The same stars circling in the night?
Eat the same fish in foreign harbors?
Breathe the same air? Sail across
These oceans only to discover
Our own island's other shore?

Let oceans spill their green from off
The edges of the earth, and let
The curving plain unbend itself
Behind the mountains. Put wind back
Into the cheeks of demons. Voice,
Pronounce your reasonable desire
And sing the round earth flat again!

Profitable, poisonous, and purely American –
it was Columbus who discovered it
on reaching China, noticing the leaves
in a canoe. He sent his men ashore
to find the Great Khan's palace. They returned
to tell of squatting natives who drank smoke.

Rolfe smuggled seeds to cold, bankrupt Virginia.
When he returned years later, all the streets
were planted with the crop, the marketplace
and churchyards overgrown. Grim ministers
preached harvest from the pulpit and stood out
among the fields at night to guard their tithes.

More valuable than silver, worth ten times
the price of peppercorn. In Africa
six rolls could buy a man. The ships would reach
Virginia stocked with slaves or English wives
while every year the farms moved farther west
abandoning their dry, exhausted fields.

Tenacious, fertile, rank as any weed,
Linnaeus counted forty thousand seeds
inside one pod. *Miraculus*, he wrote,
the cure for toothache, shingles, running sores
or, pushed by bellows through a patient's lung,
the panacea of the alchemists.

Fragrant, prophylactic, and medicinal,
Pepys chewed it during the Great Plague.
It cost a fortune, but it saved his life.
Later he spent an afternoon to watch

a surgeon kill a cat with just one drop
of the quintessence of Virginia leaf.

...But when a bear was killed, tobacco smoke
was blown into his throat to soothe the spirit.
The elders smoked and chanted in a trance.
The Mayans blew the smoke to the four corners
of the world. It was a gift from God,
profitable, poisonous, and purely American.

BIX BEIDERBECKE (1903-1931)

January, 1926

China Boy.   Lazy Daddy.   Cryin' All Day.
He dreamed he played the notes so slowly that
they hovered in the air above the crowd
and shimmered like a neon sign. But no,
the club stayed dark, trays clattered in the kitchen,
people drank and went on talking. He watched
the smoke drift from a woman's cigarette
and slowly circle up across the room
until the ceiling fan blades chopped it up.
A face, a young girl's face, looked up at him,
the stupid face of small-town innocence.
He smiled her way and wondered who she was.
He looked again and saw the face was his.

He woke up then. His head still hurt from drinking,
Jimmy was driving. Tram was still asleep.
Where were they anyway? Near Davenport?
There was no distance in these open fields –
only time, time marked by a farmhouse
or a barn, a tin-topped silo or a tree,
some momentary silhouette against
the endless, empty fields of snow.
He lit a cigarette and closed his eyes.
The best years of his life! The Boring 'Twenties.
He watched the morning break across the snow.
Would heaven be as white as Iowa?

THE MAD NUN

for Alexander Theroux

The convent yard seems larger than before
    when late last night he stood a moment
        on Paul's unsteady shoulders

and saw a garden in the moonlight
    full of flowerbeds and orange trees
        around a green-rimmed, empty pond.

Now the paths extend for miles, disappearing
    only in the gloom of trees
        that run along a wall of hedges.

At first the dreamer travels with
    his classmates, but one
        by one they drop away. Paul

transformed into a rosebush when he trips
    on a gardener's shovel. James
        sinks unresistingly into the green

surface of the pond and swims away
    a goldfish. Ernie, whose
        mother warned him when he swore,

steps off the gravel path and blends
    into the ivy, sobbing
        as his hair grows

long and green curling up a tree,
    and slowly the survivor realizes
        that everything growing in this garden

was once a schoolboy – the battered statues,
    the drooping trees, the quiet
        vines climbing up the wall.

Even the spider suspended at the entrance
    of the arbor sits trapped
        like a housefly on his web.

"How do I get out of here?"
    he begs the statues near the pond
        who cannot leave their perpetual

transfixion: Francis in ecstasy
    among the duckweed and beatific
        Dominic who smiles at the bird bath.

But it is always too late.
    A horrible laugh comes
        from behind the Grotto of Our Lady,

and then he knows that the mad nun
    everyone hears about
        has seen him in the garden.

He scrambles down the path, hearing
    her heavy, square-toed shoes
        scuff the ground behind him,

and runs between the hedges – until,
    hidden in the oleander, he hears nothing
        but his own heart beating from exertion

and thinks he has lost her. But suddenly
    he sees a flash of black
        and white behind the bushes.

There is never time to run away
    before her long, white hands
        reach out and shake him

awake, shivering in a damp bed,
    listening to the rain
        drive nails into the roof,

waiting hours
    for the humiliating
        light of dawn.

THE MEMORY

Don't listen to it. This memory
is like a snatch of an old song
in the back of your head: something
you heard years ago. Pay
attention to it now, and it
sticks forever, just out of reach,
getting louder all the time
until you swear you know the words.
Don't fool yourself. You know by now
you can't remember where it's from,
and all you'll ever get for searching
is just the sense of having left
something important in a place
you can't get back to. Ignore it.
You've never been there, never had
anything to lose, and whatever
comfort you remember in the words
is an illusion, just like the hack
who wrote it wanted there to be.
Turn on the radio and listen
to someone else's loneliness.

Every night I wake and find myself
Alone in this strange bedroom. Always puzzled,
I walk into the hallway, blinking at the lights
And somehow know I'm on the highest floor
Of an enormous mansion full of people.
Then leaning on the banister I hear
The noise of a party down below,
And sad, slow music drifting up the stairwell
Like one last waltz that an exhausted band
Will play to satisfy an audience
That won't go home. Curious, I descend
The elegantly curving staircase, finding
Each floor darker and more crowded, people
Everywhere: on the landing, in the corridors,
Some staring, others arguing, most so drunk
They don't even notice that I'm there.

Then someone calls, "Mary, come down, come down,
And dance with us!" I try to answer him,
But it's so dark and crowded I can't see
The bottom yet, and I keep walking down
Until the music, laughter, cheap perfume,
The shouting people, all the smoke from cigarettes
Makes me so dizzy I could faint, and still
He calls me, "Mary, come down, come down,"
And as I reach for him, the voices pause,
The music stops, and there is nothing there
But one voice laughing in another room.

MY SECRET LIFE

*"As a rule, the obscurity of a myth does not
reside in its form of expression. The obscurity
belongs in part to the mystery of its origins."*
— DENIS DE ROUGEMONT

I.

"I had from youth an excellent memory
    so that even now I recollect,
to an astonishing degree, the face,
    colour, stature, thighs, and backside
of every woman I have had, the clothes
    they wore, the houses and the rooms
in which I took them, where the furniture
    was placed, or where an open window
hung with white curtains moving in the wind
    allowed the light to enter.
I still see them now. Therefore I begin."

II.

These memoirs are entirely pornographic,
    an endless travelogue through a country
where no one wants to linger, where every church
    and palace sounds identical,
and the obligatory portrait of the Madonna
    found in each alcove is indistinguishable
from all the others, except in some small touch —
    an apple in the Infant's hand,
a slice of landscape seen above the windowsill,
    or farmers working in a distant field
ignored by both the Virgin and the Child.

And yet his recollections never leave
     this single theme, as if to prove
a secret life eludes the public one.
     His mother is merely a detail
in the background like a tiny piece of bric-à-brac
     in a dark and overdecorated room;
his father introduced for little else
     than dying, all the family recalled
only for the legacies it left,
     dead names on the deeds that left him rich,
a man of other people's property.

III.

Now no one ever dies in his own memoirs,
     but is it wrong to expect
some sort of ending? Some proof, however tenuous,
     that living has a purpose?
No tragic insights or comic resolutions
     mark the periods of this life
for everything is pornographic
     in the purest sense: where all
the episodes are interchangeable,
     the rooms and beds the same, each character
exactly like the next, and had the author
     by some Priapic miracle been able
to perform these conquests in the successive
     hours of a single week,
not one page or paragraph would change.

Therefore anonymity was appropriate.
    For what he explored those years
was no more personal than the anatomy
    of its participants, and his depravity
the innocent cruelty of children
    in a world where the adults
are permanently somewhere else –
    a repetitious, boyhood fantasy
where an endless succession of cousins
    visiting for the holidays
sneaks upstairs into the master bedroom
    to dress in their parents' clothes
and play a part they don't quite understand.

IV.

No other details of your life survive,
    and so your secret will be kept
forever. Now you are only what you wanted
    to be: a scholar of seduction,
certainly more the antiquarian than lover,
    and these pages catalogue a life's
accumulation of encounters with the same obsessiveness
    an eccentric would bestow
on a collection of exotic stamps: clipped,
    soaked, separated, and arranged
by year and origin neatly in an album
    until it is almost unbelievable
that every one could bring a human message.

THE END

I.

Bosch painted it. Van Eyck, Angelico,
and others. Even those without genius
could show us what they saw. These primitives
where one painting does as well as any other
in showing what still matters.

They knew, as we hardly do, that the world
is an uninhabitable place, temporary at best,
the delicate balance between eternities,
and given the light of the last morning
they could portray it as it truly is
without the covering of grass, of clouds, or weather:
only a stony plain bound by sharp grey mountains
where a crowd has waked to find itself
stripped, possessionless, abandoned to the sky.

Naked they cannot hide the sins which flesh
has grown accustomed to. The glutton's paunch,
the lover's white and vulnerable thigh.
Some raise their fists against the slate-grey sky,
but most look wildly about or stare
at the cool and unapproachable mountains
waiting in the distance.

Hell is their proud city turned to flame.
And now they stand outside the gates and watch
the gentle towers and parapets scorched black
and in the barren field beyond the wall
the resurrection of the shrouded dead.

And, if there is no hope, there is at least
the dignity of their despair.

II.

                    Last night
I dreamed the end had come. Silent, impotent,
invisible as air, I stood by in
a hundred places: a stranger's house,
a city street, an office and a garden —
and like a sleeper shaken from a dream
I witnessed what I could not understand.
A woman washing dishes at a sink
looked out her window calmly as she heard
something unexpected in the air.
Men on the sidewalk, drivers in the street
observed the weather in a cloudless sky
and kept on going. In an office clerks
and secretaries glanced up at the clock
without remembering the time. I saw
the same cold profile everywhere at once —
a pale face looking up against the light,
then bending down again indifferently,
only this dull reflex of acceptance,
then nothing else, nothing ever again.

· IV ·

JOURNEYS

IN SUNLIGHT

"an Italy of the mind"

—WALLACE STEVENS

AN EMIGRÉ IN AUTUMN

I.

Walking down the garden path
From the house you do not own,
Once again you think of how
Cool the autumns were at home.
Dressed as if you had just left
The courtyard of the summer palace,
Walk the boundaries of the park,
Count the steps you take each day –
Miles that span no distances,
Journeys in sunlight toward the dark.

Sit and watch the daylight play
Idly on the tops of leaves
Glistening overhead in autumn's
Absolute dominion.
Nothing lost by you excels
These empires of sunlight.
But even here the subtle breeze
Plots with underlying shadows.
One gust of wind and suddenly
The sun is falling from the trees.

INSTRUCTIONS FOR THE AFTERNOON

I.

Leave the museums, the comfortable rooms,
the safe distractions of the masterpiece.
The broken goddesses have lost their voice,
the martyr's folded hands no longer bless.
Footsteps echo through the palaces
where no one lives. Consider what you've come for.

Leave the museums. Find the dark churches
in back towns that history has forgotten,
the unimportant places the powerful ignore
where commerce knows no profit will be made.
Sad hamlets at the end of silted waterways,
dry mountain villages where time
is the thin shadow of an ancient tower
that moves across the sundazed pavement of the square
and disappears each evening without trace.

Make the slow climb up the winding alleys.
Walk between houses shuttered close for midday
and overhear the sound of other lives,
the conversations in the language you
will never learn. Make the long ascent
up to the grey stone chapel on the hillside
when summer is a furnace open to the world,
and pause there breathless in the blinding sun
only one moment, then enter.

For this
is how it must be seen to understand:
by walking from the sunlight into darkness,
by groping down the aisle
as your wet skin cools and your eyes adjust,
by finding what you've come for thoughtlessly,
shoved off into a corner, almost lost
among the spectacle of gold and purple.

Here in the half-light, covered by the years
it will exist. And wait,
wait like a mirror in an empty room
whose resolutions are invisible
to anyone but you. Wait like the stone
face of a statue waits, forever frozen
or poised in the moment before action.

II.

But if the vision fails, and the damp air
stinks of summer must and disrepair,
if the worn steps rising to the altar
lead nowhere but to stone, this, too, could be
the revelation — but of a destiny
fixed as the graceless frescoes on the wall —

the grim and superannuated gods
who rule this shadow-land of marble tombs,
bathed in its green suboceanic light.
Not a vision to pursue, and yet
these insufficiencies make up the world.
Strange how all journeys come to this: the sun
bright on the unfamiliar hills, new vistas
dazzling the eye, the stubborn heart unchanged.

Noon – and the shadows of the trees
have fallen from the branches. The frail
blue butterflies still flutter hungrily
among the weeds, and a few pale flowers
climb up the yellow hill and fade away.
The scarred brown lizards lie immobile
in the dust. A line of ants
picks clean the carcass of a frog.

Only the smallest things survive
in this exhausted land the gods
so long ago abandoned. Time
and rain have washed the hero's face
from off the statue. The sundial
stands perpetually in shade.

The bankrupt palace still remains
beyond the wall that summer builds,
doors bolted shut, the roof caved in,
the ancient family without heirs,
and one half-blind old man who sits
each day beside the empty pond
mumbling to himself in dialect.
The village boys throw stones at him,
but he will never leave, and there
is no one left who knows if he
was once the servant or the sire.

SONG FROM A COURTYARD WINDOW

for Harry Craig (1921-1978)

This was the only music we had hoped for:
something to make us close our eyes and lose
the courtyard full of people, silence all
the conversations at the other tables
and stop us from believing that we heard
the sunlight burning in the open sky.
Yes, and for a moment we heard nothing
but the rush of cool water underground
moving from the mountains to the hills
into these fountains splashing in the sun.

And listening we did not wonder
that all the buildings melted to a field,
off in some high country — a landscape we
had never seen before, nor had imagined,
a bitter landscape that two thousand years
of pastoral could not obscure or soften:
a wide dry field under the sun at noon
where tall brown grass was bending in a wind
filled with the sharp smell of a single weed
that had marked this season here for centuries.
The same wind drifting over the same land
forever and forever. And the same
uncomprehending melody still coming
from somewhere out of sight, from what small shade
the place could offer, a thirsty man
singing praises to the heat, a song

to celebrate the dust, the weeds, the weather,
the misery of living here alone.

What did the vision mean? We did not ask.
It was where the voice had brought us, nothing more,
and while the voice was there we did not wonder
that a bare field, scorched by a hot wind
from between mountains, could make us forget
everywhere and everyone else. Or why
before we questioned it, it should be over.

But no, it never lasts. The alluring voice
cracks reaching for a high note that would join
two passages; the fingers stumble on a piece
of brilliant bridgework. Bows scrape.
The second part falls half a step behind.
And the sunlight fades. The distant hills
become drearily familiar. Other voices,
the usual ones, start up behind us.
A moment's pause, then nothing more.

                                                    And yet
wasn't this the purpose of our listening:
to sit in the same place with our eyes open
and know that we have moved? That finally
we've woken up into the place from which
we've always woken out of, that strange place
that's always changing, constantly drifting
between the visible and invisible,
that place that we must stumble onto, now
as an unkept garden,

now as an arbor leading to a house,
a half-shut door, a carpet underfoot,
shuttered windows and a hallway
leading to a bedroom we cannot enter
without waking.
                    But wait. Does it vanish too?
Or does it stay there, shut forever, always
waiting for the footsteps turning in the hall?

THE JOURNEY, THE ARRIVAL
AND THE DREAM

I.

You're here. Finally. After hours in a hot compartment
on the slow train coming through the mountains.
And everywhere the same crowd of brown-toothed men
and fools in uniform stood smoking in the shade,
waiting on the platform as if each train
might bring the fortune missing from their lives.

As the local dragged
from one such dusty station to another,
did it cross your mind that this same village
lost in the dry mountains was all
there ever would be, that your life was bound
by the four walls of your compartment, and the women,
their brats, and blank-eyed daughters were freer
than you would ever be again? That the pale clerk
behind the counter at the last connection,
looking at his watch, nodding at everything you said,
had not understood a word?
       No matter. You are here:
a woman still young enough to feel pain
as undeserved. And no time left for bitterness.
The car is waiting. One short drive and then
your final destination,
an ancient house on a yellow hill. Reality
more sinister than any clerk's revenge.

II.

It is late afternoon,
and you are standing in a room where the servant
has already left and shut the door. The wood-framed windows

look down a sloping valley somewhat bleached in haze,
and you lean against the windowpanes amazed
that these mountains and the mountains there beyond them,
dark green blurring into blue, then into grey and black,
could have been the obstacles you passed.
Journeys are the despair before discovery,
you hope, wondering if this one ends.

Emptying your pockets on the dresser, notice
how carefully you put down all the useless keys
and currency you've brought from home, so terrified
of scratching the patina of the varnished wood
that innocently reflects the lamp, your hand, the curtains,
and the badly painted cherubs on the ceiling.
who ignore you. Light a cigarette and watch
the lazy smoke creep up and tickle them
to no effect and realize you don't
belong here in their world where everything
is much too good for you, and though the angels
will say nothing, they watch everything you do.

III.

But you are also in another room
finishing a letter in a language
you don't understand, your dark hair pulled
back loosely in a bun, and the crucifix
you bring everywhere set upon the desk
like a photograph from home.
                              Long ago,
had someone told you this would happen,

you would have thought then only of escape,
of returning to yourself. Instead you feel calm,
relaxing in this dying body
like a swimmer on a sunlit beach, and death,
the light you cannot look directly into, seems
as illuminating and warm.
                                    Now the hand, your hand,
is sealing up the envelope, and you turn to face
an old man in a dark-red uniform.
He nods. You speak affectionately.
And word by word the language too becomes
familiar. But still you wonder,
who is he? Husband? Servant? Ancient friend?
Too late. He takes the envelope and leaves.
The door has closed and from outside you hear
his footsteps fade into the murmuring
of swallows in the eaves.
                                    Where do they come from?
Why can't you see them from the window?
No use to look. There's only this blue patch
of sky and endlessly empty afternoon,
where the light is fading.
                                    Close your eyes. Accept
that some things must remain invisible.
Somewhere in the valley a grey fox
is moving through the underbrush. Old men
are harvesting the grapes. And the dark swallows
you cannot see are circling in the sunlight
slowly gliding downward in the valley
as if the light would last forever.

· V ·

"Amor y vispera de amor y recuerdos intolerables"

"Love and the imminence of love and the intolerable remembering"

—JORGE LUIS BORGES,
"Matthew XXV 30"
(translated by Alastair Reid)

V

The flowers sent here by mistake,
signed with a name that no one knew,
are turning bad. What shall we do?
Our neighbor says they're not for her,
and no one has a birthday near.
We should thank someone for the blunder.
Is one of us having an affair?
At first we laugh, and then we wonder.

The iris was the first to die,
enshrouded in its sickly-sweet
and lingering perfume. The roses
fell one petal at a time,
and now the ferns are turning dry.
The room smells like a funeral,
but there they sit, too much at home,
accusing us of some small crime,
like love forgotten, and we can't
throw out a gift we've never owned.

CUCKOOS

I heard them only once. Climbing in the mountains,
I stopped to rest a moment on a ledge
and listen to the river distantly below –
when suddenly they began to call each other
back and forth from trees across the valley,
invisible in pinetops but bright and clear
like the ring of crystal against crystal.
I didn't move but lay there wondering
what they were like, amazed that folklore
had made their cry the omen of betrayal.

So now, reading how the Chinese took their call
to mean *Pu ju kuei, pu ju kuei* –
Come home again, you must come home again –
I understand at last what they were telling me
not then, back in that high, green valley,
but here, this evening, in the memory of it,
returned by these birds that I have never seen.

PHOTOGRAPH OF MY MOTHER
AS A YOUNG GIRL

She wasn't looking
when they took this picture:
sitting on the grass
in her bare feet
wearing a cotton dress,
she stares off to the side
watching something on the lawn
the camera didn't catch.
What was it?
A ladybug? A flower?
Judging from her expression,
possibly nothing at all,
or else
the lawn was like a mirror,
and she sat watching herself,
wondering who she was
and how she came to be there
sitting in this backyard,
wearing a cheap, white dress,
imagining that tomorrow
would be like all her yesterdays,
while her parents chatted
and watched, as I do
years later,
too distantly to interfere.

HIS THREE WOMEN

I.

Her frequent letters are like childhood friends:
He understands their silences. No deep
Mystery clouds her cursory approach.
She loves him openly and wants him back.
In the mornings when he tries to work,
Everything that happens – from the way
The sunlight draws its silhouettes from dust
Drifting in the window to some turn
Of phrase he comes across while reading – makes
Him think of her.
                        How maddening to have
A constant woman constantly in mind.
Yet how much worse when she can only fill
The waking mind, an obsession in the morning,
A memory at night, an absence in his dreams.
There is every reason he should love her
Except that love will never come from reason.

II.

Her short, reluctant letters seldom come,
And their misspellings tell him very little,
But with the solid scholarship of lust
He finds a dozen hints in every line
To justify his loyalty.
                        More beautiful
Than blushing reason can approach in comfort,
Her form refutes each judgment of her mind
That he has made. He doesn't understand her

But has explored his memories and studies
The single photograph which he possesses
Like the scene of a murder
Whose mysteries have never been resolved.

III.

Somewhere not far away
A dark-haired woman he has never met
Unpacks the last of her heavy trunks
Wondering sadly what she left behind
And in the stillness of a settled past
Forgets the future's infidelity.
Nervously she marks out her domain
And walks around the newly rented rooms
In which the unexpected
Presses like the air outside her windows,
Moving invisibly through every crack
Into a life resumed in this new city.
Suddenly she catches her reflection
In the silent, unconfiding mirror –
A lonely woman in an empty room.
She turns away, but sick of indecision,
Accepts its present tense as permanent,
And falling on the unmade bed, her hand,
Which has not touched him yet, turns out the light.

PARTS OF SUMMER WEATHER

The window open and the summer air
drifts slowly through the darkened room.
The curtains lift enough to see
a starless night and heavy moon.

Upstairs a radio plays out
the songs we've overheard together
so many nights now that they seem
like one more part of summer weather.

And under darkness and the breeze
with sheets and blankets stripped away
we lie in silence saying more
than anything we hoped to say.

And yet I wake an hour later,
reach out and find myself alone.
No words spoken, no message left,
the room so quiet, and you gone.

VIEW FROM THE SECOND STORY

There were no colors in the sunset.
Rain had been coming down for hours,
and the winter sky was a bright grey
against the windowpanes. Lights were coming on
in all the other houses, but here
only weak sunlight from the rain-streaked glass
dissolving in the shadows of the furniture.
How easily the room comes back again.
I can still feel the cold, still hear the cars
streaking down the rainy avenues below us.
You are in the bedroom, sleeping, or crying.
I don't know which. Am I afraid to look?
And I am still standing at the wide window
looking for something beyond the dark rows
of winter trees and houses, feeling the cold air
that somehow finds its way between the cracks
of any windowsill, and I am waiting,
listening to the rain while the air which seemed
invisible turns gradually to black.

THE END OF A SEASON

I wanted to tell you how I walked tonight
down the hillside to the lake
after the storm had blown away
and say how everything suddenly seemed so clear
against the sparkling, rain-soaked streets
cold and bright as starlight.

l wanted to wake you up, despite the hour,
and drag you out into the dark
crisp air to feel the end of winter,
the cold we cursed so long
slipping away – and suddenly so precious
now that it was leaving.

But there is no one to come back to now,
only the night, its wind and rain, the chill
magnificence of its borrowed light,
the touch of this impossible season.

THE SUNDAY NEWS

Looking for something in the Sunday paper,
I flipped by accident through *Local Weddings*,
Yet missed the photograph until I saw
Your name among the headings.

And there you were, looking almost unchanged,
Your hair still long, though now long out of style,
And you still wore that stiff and serious look
You called a smile.

I felt as though we sat there face to face.
My stomach tightened. I read the item through.
It said too much about both families,
Too little about you.

Finished at last, I threw the paper down,
Stung by jealousy, my mind aflame,
Hating this man, this stranger whom you loved,
This printed name.

And yet I clipped it out to put away
Inside a book like something I might use,
A scrap I knew I wouldn't read again
But couldn't bear to lose.

THE COUNTRY WIFE

She makes her way through the dark trees
Down to the lake to be alone.
Following their voices on the breeze,
She makes her way. Through the dark trees
The distant stars are all she sees.
They cannot light the way she's gone.
She makes her way through the dark trees
Down to the lake to be alone.

The night reflected on the lake,
The fire of stars changed into water.
She cannot see the winds that break
The night reflected on the lake
But knows they motion for her sake.
These are the choices they have brought her:
The night reflected on the lake,
The fire of stars changed into water.

FOUR SPEECHES FOR PYGMALION

I.

I wished to carve a face that understood
Our life's few dismal certainties. The face
Of an eternal witness trapped in time.
But cutting her from stone, I let each line
Blend with the line before it, and the pain
I had intended never reached her face.
Now she is finished, standing in the room
Smiling almost imperceptibly, one hand
Stretched out as if to touch the spectator.
What waits beyond the arrogance of stone?
I cannot tell. Nor can she answer.

II.

You were the light, hidden in the stone,
Never the stone itself. Which of the cuttings
Swept in the corner could be part of you
And not the shadow my thought lost in birth?
You do not feel the hand that made you.
Stone endures but without memory.

III.

Now it is nearly midnight, and I sit
By myself in the dark, unable to work,
Unwilling to leave, wondering if I
Should speak to her again. Night forgets
The futility of rhetoric to stone.
Forgives the confidence that made me think

I could force stone into a single shape
And satisfy ambition like a debt
Pretending there was permanence in love.

IV.

What do you want? Is something left to give?
The room still dark you stand beside me
Demanding as the silence after thunder.

THE ROOM UPSTAIRS

Come over to the window for a moment –
I want to show you something. Do you see
The one hill without trees? The dust-brown one
Above the highway? That's how it all looked
When I first came – no watered lawns or trees,
Just open desert, pale green in the winter,
Then brown and empty till the end of fall.
I never look in mirrors any more,
Or if I do, I just stare at the tie
I'm knotting, and it's easy to pretend
I haven't changed. But how can I ignore
The way these hills were cut up into houses?
I always thought the desert would outlive me.

How did I get started on this subject?
I'm really not as morbid as I sound.
We hardly know each other, but I think
You'll like it here – the college isn't far,
And this old house, like me, still has its charms.
I chose the site myself and drew the plans –
A modern house, all open glass and stone,
The rooms squared off and cleared of memory.
No wonder Mother hated the idea.
I had to wait until she died to build.
It was her money after all.

                                        No,
I never married, never had the time
Or inclination to. Still, getting older,
One wonders…not so much about a wife –

No mystery there – but about a son.
What part of me might have been realized in him?
My face? My voice? My vanity?

                              I guess
I always looked for one among my students
And found too many. Never look for what
You truly want. It comes too easily,
And then you never value it enough –
Until it's gone – gone like these empty hills
And all the years I spent ignoring them.

There was a boy who lived here years ago –
Named David – a clever, handsome boy
Who thought he was a poet. That was back
When I still dreamed of writing. I recall
The night we met. How sure I felt that he
Would spur me on. How innocent we were.
How fatuous. He was a student here –
In those rare moments when he chose to study,
But climbing was the only thing he cared for.
It's strange how clearly I remember him.
He lived here off and on almost two years –
In the same room that you are moving into.
You'll like the room. David always did.

Once during a vacation he went off
With friends to climb El Capitan. They took
A girl with them. But it's no easy thing
To climb three thousand feet of granite,
And halfway up, she froze, balanced on a ledge.

They nearly killed themselves to get her down.
At one point David had to wedge himself
Into a crevice, tie down to a rock,
And lower her by rope to another ledge.
When it was over, they were furious.
They drove her back, and he
Surprised me, coming here instead of home.

His clothes were torn, his hands and face cut up.
I went upstairs for bandages, but he
Wanted to shower first. When he called me in,
I watched him standing in the steamy bathroom,
His naked body shining from the water,
Carefully drying himself with a towel.
Then suddenly he threw it down and showed me
Where the ropes had cut into his skin.
It looked as if he had been branded,
Wounds deep enough to hide your fingers in.
I felt like holding him but couldn't bear it.
I helped him into bed and spent the night
Sitting in this room, too upset to sleep.
And on the morning after he drove home.

He graduated just a few months later,
And then went off to Europe where he wrote me
Mainly about beer halls and mountain trips.
I wrote that they would be the death of him.
That spring his mother phoned me when he fell.
I wonder if you know how strange it feels
When someone so much younger than you dies?

And, if I tell you something, will you not
Repeat it? It is something I don't understand.

The night he died I had a dream. I dreamt
That suddenly the room was filled with light,
Not blinding but the soft whiteness that you see
When heavy snow is falling in the morning,
And I awoke to see him standing here,
Waiting in the doorway, his arms outstretched.
"I've come back to you," he said. "Look at me.
Let me show you what I've done for you."

And only then I saw his skin was bruised,
Torn in places, crossed by deep red welts,
But this time everywhere – as if his veins
Had pushed up to the surface and spilled out.
And there was nothing in his body now,
Nothing but the voice that spoke to me,
And this cold white light pouring through the room.

I stared at him. His skin was bright and pale.
"Why are you doing this to me?" I asked.
"Please, go away."
                    "But I've come back to you.
I'm cold. Just hold me. I'm so very cold."

What else could I have done but hold him there?
I took him in my arms – he was so light –
And held him in the doorway listening.
Nothing else was said or lost it seemed.
I waited there while it grew dark again,

And he grew lighter, slipping silently away
Like snow between my fingers, and was gone.

That's all there is to say. I can't explain it,
And now I'm sorry to have bored you so.
It's getting late. You know the way upstairs.
But no, of course not. Let me show you to your room.

THE LETTER

And in the end, all that is really left
Is a feeling – strong and unavoidable –
That somehow we deserved something better.
That somewhere along the line things
Got fouled up. And that letter from whoever's
In charge, which certainly would have set
Everything straight between us and the world,
Never reached us. Got lost somewhere.
Possibly mislaid in some provincial station.
Or sent by mistake to an old address
Whose new tenant put it on her dresser
With the curlers and the hairspray forgetting
To give it to the landlord to forward.
And we still wait like children who have sent
Two weeks' allowance far away
To answer an enticing advertisement
From a crumbling, yellow magazine,
Watching through years as long as a childhood summer,
Checking the postbox with impatient faith
Even on days when mail is never brought.

The carnival is over. The high tents,
the palaces of light, are folded flat
and trucked away. A three-time loser yanks
the Wheel of Fortune off the wall. Mice
pick through the garbage by the popcorn stand.
A drunken giant falls asleep beside
the juggler, and the Dog-Faced Boy sneaks off
to join the Serpent Lady for the night.
Wind sweeps ticket stubs along the walk.
The Dead Man loads his coffin on a truck.
Off in a trailer by the parking lot
the radio predicts tomorrow's weather
while a clown stares in a dressing mirror,
takes out a box, and peels away his face.

Lives of the Great Composers

This poem is cast as a verbal fugue in a form suggested by a poem of Weldon Kees's. All the historical incidents described are true.

Bix Beiderbecke

Leon Bismarck Beiderbecke, better known as "Bix," was a famous jazz cornetist of the 'Twenties and is generally considered the first white musician to make a significant contribution to jazz.

A Short History of Tobacco

Tobacco (genus *Nicotiana*) was originally found only in the Americas, where natives used it in sacred ceremonies. All the incidents mentioned in this poem are true.

My Secret Life

My Secret Life is an eleven-volume sexual autobiography published privately in 1888. The author, a Victorian gentleman of private means, has never been identified.

DANA GIOIA was born in Los Angeles in 1950. He received B.A. and M.B.A. degrees from Stanford University. His poems have appeared in many magazines including *The Paris Review, Poetry, The New Yorker,* and *The Hudson Review.* In 1984 he was chosen by *Esquire* in their first Register of "Men and Women under 40 Who are Changing the Nation." An executive with a major American corporation, Dana Gioia lives with his wife outside New York City.

Book designed by Tree Swenson
Galliard type designed by Matthew Carter